# missives

by alicia wirt-fox

ISBN: 1-930337-44-2

Published by

Codhill Press

New Paltz, NY

Book and Cover Design:
Alicia Fox

To
the Enchanted

## Comprehension

Flesh, bone, nail, hair,
Tooth, nerve and sinew.

Matter stuffed connectors.
Dense passages.

Hold incomplete transmissions,
Immanently waiting.

To comprehend.

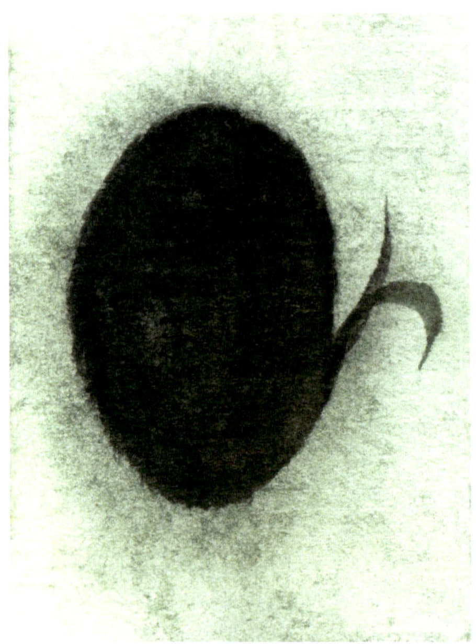

## Crush

Old, gnarled knob — collected, useless stuff,
Is pulverized.

Transfigured into glorious dirt
—Dirt with worms and bugs.

Humbly breathing,
feeding,
scratching,
squirming.

Dark womb waiting.

To receive the unforeseen.

My dead matter — resurrected.

Crushed.

## Hallowed

I am made hallow
by your breath

Expanding—
rendering me
transparent

To expose a
lattice work
of bone

An intimate space
without ceiling

No walls.

## Pumice Stone

It hit me, today
After our conversation
That my life is a pumice stone.

I undress
and run head long
into these forces.

I let them rub me raw.

And break me down.

Until there is nothing left.

## Form

Stones set in concrete,
          fixed form.

Mountains are fluid in comparison.

Light punctured structures
          aerate obscure spaces.

Emancipation of the natural.

Worlds built of space and light.
Whole waves forever related.

Without parts.

## Night Light

Night light
illuminating messages
held beyond my scope.

Uncovered by incandescence
matter is shown to be
incomplete.

Emulating fictions,
of past or future
happenings.

Fruitless mementos.
Honoring no one or no thing.

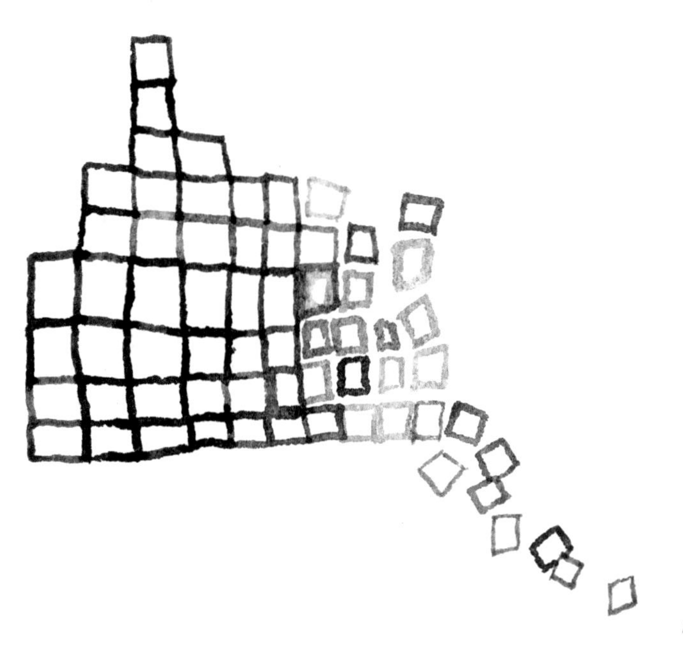

## Revelation

The great revelations of this world are always lost.  
Again and again.

We uncover them in moments when silence reigns.  
But then again, we forget.

Intelligence is given and taken away  
—like a stack of blocks piled high into the sky!

And then, blocks turn into rocks  
—tumbling down into the every day clamor.

If only we could remember what we have been given.

## Crevasses

Monumental.

Memories held in rock.
No escaping
malleable maneuvering.

What can remain?

The enchanted live in caves
and crevasses.

Hidden and eternal.

Magical emptiness
sustains.

A food like no other.

## The Turn

Innocence
Turns and turns

And turns
Around the center

Waiting.

Just waiting.
With no designs.

Relinquishing my will
For Thine.

Abandoning logic
I embrace
your Word.

...and Hide
my face
in happiness.

## This and That

Sometimes mind gets stuck at that place.
You know—that gap between this and that.
It sinks between the here and there.
Glimpsing at the glimmering gone, gone, gone.

No holding the gone. No holding on to not.
You know—that gap between this and that.

And yet I dive between the here and there.
To enter the never been seen.
And re-emerge in a state of wonder.

## Surrounded

Truth hides in the measureless.
Where,
Messages mingle between earth and star,
And
Hover in the space between.

Here,
These grains are ground
Into
the imperceptible,
And
Infused into the blackness
which
embed these shining points.

We wander towards these tangibles,
Stupid and drunk.
And
Do not see
That we are
Surrounded.

## Grey

Worried that the light will fade
without an eye to see its passing.

And the last utterance
will be inaudible.

Worried that we will not notice
the fade from green to grey.

Worried that we will not recognize
that She is gone
and that we are alone—
wondering who we are.

## Solicitude

Total solicitude requires solitude.

Servitude encased in emptiness.

This is an anti-prison.

Where everything evaporates.

Except remembrance,
in a quiet space.

A perpetual Sunday.

Facing nothing but,
transparent night.

## Thank you

To D.A. for listening and ushering this book out into the world.

To F.S. for listening and reading my poems.

To S.C. for listening and bearing with my long silences.

To A.B. for teaching me everything he knows about book design and for insisting that I eat lunch.

To S.F. for the support and encouragement to "just keep going."

Alicia Wirt-Fox was born in Chicago, Illinois. She received her BFA from Parsons School of Design and her MFA from Yale University School of Art. She has exhibited her paintings in numerous group and solo exhibitions throughout the United States and Europe. She is a recipient of the 19th Annual Richard Kelly Grant for her experimental work utilizing reflective light and color within the context of painting and sculpture. For over a decade, she has worked as a graphic designer in the publishing industry and has been involved in the development, design and creation of many books for education. *Missives* is her first book combining both her writing and images. She currently lives and works in Greenpoint, Brooklyn.